Ice Breaker

The Freezing Story of Lynne Cox

John DiConsiglio

SCHOLASTIC INC.
New York Toronto London Auckland Sydney
Mexico City New Delhi Hong Kong Buenos Aires

Cover photo
© Gabriella Miotto

Printed in the U.S.A.

ISBN 0-439-69653-4

1 2 3 4 5 6 7 8 9 10 23 12 11 10 09 08 07 06 05 04

Contents

Introduction

You jump into a swimming pool. It feels cold, right? But why? The water in the pool is about 76–80 degrees.* That's as warm as a warm summer day.

Still, your body feels cold at first. That's because your body is warmer than the water. Your body **temperature** is about 98.6 degrees*. But after a few minutes, you get used to the water.

Now say you jump into water near Antarctica. It's only 32 degrees. You feel

temperature how hot or cold something is

* *All the temperatures in this book are in degrees Fahrenheit.*

Lynne Cox takes a break near Los Angeles. She's famous for swimming long distances. She's also famous for swimming in really cold water.

very cold. But this time, you don't get used to it. And you'd better get out soon, or you'll probably die.

Unless you're Lynne Cox.

Lynne is the world's best cold-water swimmer. She swims in water that would kill anyone else. This is her story.

Lynne Cox was a great swimmer.
Just how far could she go?

1

In Cold Water

Lynne Cox grew up in New Hampshire. She learned to swim in a lake in Maine. Her family moved to California when she was 12. There, Lynne was on a swim team.

The team practiced in pools. But Lynne liked swimming in the ocean. "The ocean water makes you feel free and **weightless**," she says. "It's like you're in another world."

So Lynne joined a team that swam in the

weightless light; without any weight

Here, Lynne is 15. She has just set a new record for swimming the English Channel. The channel separates England and France.

ocean. The team swam in really long races. Lynne was one of the fastest swimmers.

The team was planning a big swim. They were going to swim 27 miles off the coast of Los Angeles. Lynne and four other kids made it. They did the swim in 12 hours and 36 minutes.

channel a body of water between two pieces of land

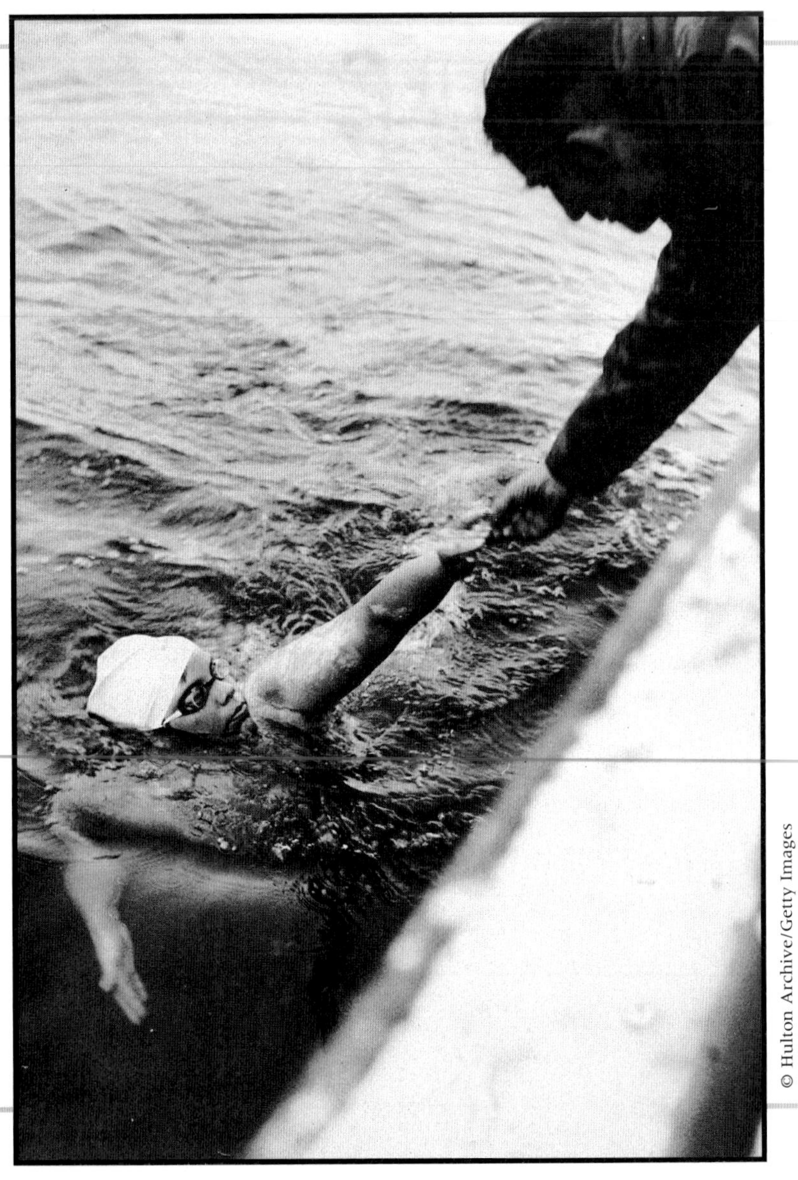

Lynne reaches for a snack while swimming the English Channel. She has to be careful. If she touches anyone, her swim doesn't count.

Next, Lynne wanted to try another big swim. She wanted to swim the English Channel. That's the body of water that separates England and France.

This swim would be about the same **distance** as the Los Angeles swim. But the water would be about 10 degrees colder.

Lynne had to get ready for the cold. She swam in the Pacific Ocean year round. It can drop to 50 degrees.

Lynne wore summer clothes in winter. At night, she left her windows open. And she slept without a blanket.

Finally, Lynne was ready. She swam the English Channel. It took her nine hours and 57 minutes. She broke both the men's **record** and the women's record. She was 15 years old.

---

distance the space between two places

record the fastest or most something has ever been done

The Big Chill

What happens to your body in freezing water?

Say it's winter and you fall into an icy river. Your body knows it's in trouble. It acts fast. It tries to take care of your heart, lungs, brain, and other **organs**.

So your body sends most of your blood to those organs. The blood keeps your organs warm. It also brings them oxygen. Without oxygen, your organs won't work.

But now hardly any blood is going to your arms or legs. Soon, you can't move them. That means you can't swim. You might drown!

But let's say you *don't* drown. You're still in trouble. Your body knows that your arms and legs need blood. So it sends them some. By now, your arms and legs are really cold. So the blood gets cold, too. Then the cold blood goes back to your heart. That can make your heart stop.

The cold blood also makes your body temperature drop. That's called **hypothermia**. You need to get out of the water and warm up. Otherwise, your heart could slow down—or even stop!

Somehow Lynne can stand freezing water. But the rest of us can't. So stay out of freezing water!

organs important parts of your body

hypothermia when someone's body temperature is much too low

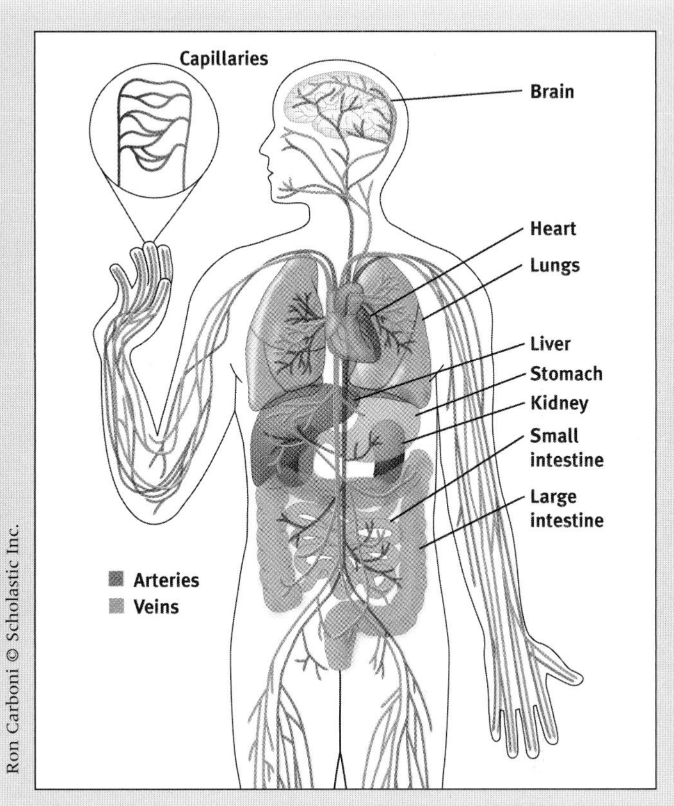

The circulatory system. Blood goes into and out of your heart. Tubes called arteries take blood *from* the heart. Veins take blood *to* the heart. Tiny tubes called capillaries connect the arteries and veins.

Lynne tried a tough swim.
And a whole country gave her support.

2

Bringing People Together

In February 1975, Lynne was 18. She was getting ready to set a new record. She planned to swim the Cook **Strait**. It's in New Zealand. Three men had crossed it. But no woman ever had.

It was a rough swim. Strong winds pushed Lynne off course. And nine-foot waves blocked her path. Lynne wanted to quit. But something happened that kept

strait a body of water that connects two larger bodies of water

her going. Lynne had a crew that followed her in a boat. A guy from a New Zealand radio station was part of the crew. He told listeners how Lynne was doing. They started calling in. They sent messages of support to Lynne.

After 12 hours, she finished the swim.

The people of New Zealand gave Lynne an idea. Her long swims could bring people together.

In 1976, Lynne came up with a plan. She would swim the Bering Strait. It's a body of water that separates Alaska from Siberia. Alaska is in the United States. And at the time, Siberia was part of a country called the Soviet Union (U.S.S.R.).

Back then, the U.S. and the U.S.S.R. were enemies. But Lynne had high hopes

© Rob Stapleton/Corbis

Lynne warms up for her Bering Strait swim in 1987. Along with extreme cold, she faced huge waves and thick fog.

for her swim. Maybe it would bring people from the two countries together.

Lynne's swim would be about five miles. The water was only 38–40 degrees. Lynne had never swum in water that cold.

But that wasn't her biggest problem. Lynne had to ask the U.S.S.R. to let her do the swim. She wrote dozens of letters. She called everyone who might help. And she kept swimming long distances. After 11 years, the U.S.S.R. said yes.

On August 7, 1987, Lynne finally swam the Bering Strait. It wasn't her longest swim. But it was her coldest so far. "It was icy cold," she said. It was like "swimming naked into a blizzard."

Lynne was the first person to cross the Bering Strait. But her greatest **challenge** was still to come.

How do you think Lynne felt when she reached the U.S.S.R.?

challenge something that is very hard to do

Wonder Woman

How can Lynne's body take the cold water?

Say you swam in very cold water. Your temperature would drop. But Lynne's does not. Her temperature rises! How does she do it? Scientists have many ideas.

First, Lynne has trained for years in cold water. Scientists think that has helped.

Second, Lynne has worked to develop large muscles. That helps, too. Muscles make heat when they move. Big muscles make more heat.

Lynne also has a little extra body fat. That helps keep her arms and legs warm. It also keeps her blood warm.

There's one more thing. Lynne is very determined. She says she has "trained her mind to achieve these swims."

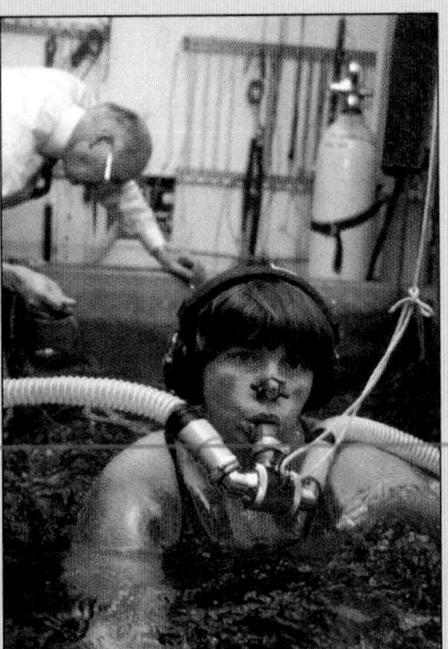

© Bill Curtsinger

As Lynne sits in cold water, scientists study how her body handles the cold.

Lynne was ready for another challenge. How about the coldest water ever?

3

Getting Ready

In 2000, Lynne started planning a new swim. She wanted to swim near Antarctica. The water there is about 32 degrees. Lynne had never swum in water that cold. No one knew what her body would do.

Lynne spent two years getting ready. She trained harder than ever. And she thought of ways to stay warm in the icy water.

Lynne studied animals that live in the

Antarctic. Penguins and seals have fat to keep them warm. So Lynne started eating more food. She gained 12 pounds.

Penguins also have feathers to keep them warm. Lynne couldn't grow feathers. So she grew her hair long. She would pile it under her swim cap. It would help keep her head warm.

That was important. You can lose a lot of heat through your head. So Lynne also planned to swim with her head above water. It's really hard to swim that way. So Lynne had to make her neck stronger.

Lynne was also building other muscles. Big muscles make you strong. They also make more heat. Lynne worked out five days a week. She lifted weights. She walked five miles a day. And she swam.

Lynne also had to protect her teeth. Teeth have tiny holes in them. Water can get in. If the water freezes, the teeth break. Lynne's dentist filled in the holes with stuff called **fluoride**.

Lynne also got special earplugs. They fit very tightly in her ears. They kept water out. Her eardrums would not freeze.

Lynne had to choose the color of her bathing suit. She did not want to look like a penguin. And she did not want to look hurt. A killer animal might attack her. So she could not wear black, white, or red.

Lynne also had to plan when to swim. In Antarctica, chunks of ice can be as big as cars. If the water is rough, the ice can kill you. So Lynne had to swim when the water was calm.

fluoride stuff put in toothpaste and water to protect your teeth

And what about after the swim? How would Lynne warm up? Again, she studied penguins. They keep warm by crowding together. After Lynne's swim, her crew would crowd around her. Lynne would put on special clothes. The clothes had pockets with little heaters in them.

Finally, Lynne was ready. She was headed for Antarctica.

Sudden Death

Here's how long people can survive cold water.

Water Temperature	Time Before You Probably Die
59 degrees	7 hours
50 degrees	3 hours
41 degrees	1 hour
32 degrees	may die instantly

reference: Transport Canada Report/Marine Safety

The biggest challenge was here.
Could Lynne's body take it?

4

Swimming to Antarctica

In December 2002, Lynne took a ship to Antarctica. She saw giant icebergs all around her. Icy winds slapped her face.

Lynne was planning to swim a mile. She would start from the ship. She'd swim to the coast of Antarctica.

Could Lynne stand the cold? She did a test swim to find out. She wanted to swim for 10 minutes. At first, she didn't think

© Gabriella Miotto

Lynne and her crew went to Antarctica in a boat called the *Orlova*. Here, she's getting ready to jump from the boat into the water.

she'd make it. The water was icy cold. She couldn't catch her breath. Lynne said, "It was like swimming through a Sno Kone."

Then a wave hit Lynne in the face. She got scared. Another wave hit her. She began to choke. She knew she'd have to put her head in the water.

© Gabriella Miotto

Once Lynne was in the water, she had to dodge icebergs. Lynne's crew followed her in a small boat to make sure she was okay.

With her head down, Lynne could swim better. It was easier to breathe. She began to feel calmer.

She kept swimming. Then she looked at her watch. Her ten minutes were up. But Lynne kept going. She swam for 22 minutes.

© Gabriella Miotto

Lynne tries to warm up after her swim. She had just become the first person in the world to swim a mile in the water off Antarctica.

Two days later, Lynne was ready to swim a mile. She and her crew picked out a spot for the swim. Her crew ran a rope through her bathing suit. They planned to pull her out if she got in trouble.

Lynne took a deep breath and leaned forward. She slipped and fell into the water. She hit face first.

She caught her breath. Then she started swimming. To stay warm, she swam as fast as she could.

She got tired quickly. She almost swam into a huge piece of ice. But she kept swimming.

Near shore, she saw some penguins. They started jumping into the water. They swam over to her.

A few minutes later, Lynne reached

shore. She had been in the water 25 minutes. And she had swum 1.22 miles.

Lynne's friends helped her back into the boat. She was shaking. Her body temperature was down to 95.5 degrees. After a few hours, Lynne warmed up.

That night, Lynne and her crew had a big party. She had done something that seemed impossible. "It was a great dream, swimming to Antarctica," Lynne said.

Lynne says that swimming to Antarctica was "a great dream." What great dreams do you have?

Glossary

challenge *(noun)* something that is very hard to do

channel *(noun)* a body of water between two pieces of land

distance *(noun)* the space between two places

fluoride *(noun)* stuff put in toothpaste and water to protect your teeth

hypothermia *(noun)* when someone's body temperature is much too low

organs *(noun)* important parts of your body

record *(noun)* the fastest or most something has ever been done

strait *(noun)* a body of water that connects two larger bodies of water

temperature *(noun)* how hot or cold something is

weightless *(adjective)* light; without any weight